HOW TO DRA

MERMAIDS, UNICORNS

AND MORE

A Fun and Step-by-Step Guide for Kids to Draw Beautiful Mermaids, Lovely Unicorns, Mythical Creatures and Many Amazing Things

How to Draw Mermaids, Unicorns and More

A Fun and Step-by-Step Guide for Kids to Draw Beautiful Mermaids, Lovely Unicorns, Mythical Creatures and Many Amazing Things

This Book Belongs to

_____

TABLE OF CONTENTS

Mermaid 1	10	Unicorn 1	62
Mermaid 2	12	Unicorn 2	64
Bubble	14	Unicorn 3	66
Octopus	16	Baby Unicorn	68
Jellyfish	18	Rainbow	70
Sea Turtle	20	Fairy	72
Tang Fish	22	Magical Dust	74
Narwhal	24	Magic Wand	76
Sea Horse	26	Mushroom House	78
Conch Shell	28	Pegasus	80
Coral	30	Golden Apple	82
Kraken	32	Alicorn	84
Pearl	34	Butterfly	86
Dolphin	36	Crystal	88
Starfish	38	Lily	90
Seaweed	40	Sun	92
Moon	42	Shooting Star	94
Seagull	44	Castle Tower	96
Whale	46	Princess	98
Crab	48	Diamond	100
Kelp	50	Crown	102
Mermaid 3	52	Dragon	104
Mermaid 4	54	Griffin	106
Merman	56	Elf	108
Trident	58	Pixie	110
Triton	60	Phoenix	112

"Hello, Young Artist!

My name is Leo, and I'm excited to share this book with you.

As an artist myself, I know how magical and thrilling it can be to create your own characters and bring them to life on paper. In this book, you'll find step-by-step guides to help you draw some of the most enchanting creatures in the world - from mystical mermaids to majestic unicorns and beyond. So grab your pencils, get comfortable, and let's explore the wonderful world of drawing together!

LEO

BEFORE YOU START

Let's talk about the black lines and gray lines in our guide.

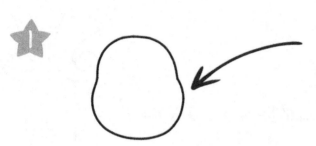

Black lines are the start of each step in your drawing adventure!

Black lines are also the new lines that you get to add to your drawing in the next steps.

Grey lines are the lines you've already drawn in previous steps.

If you come across a broken line in a step, that's a signal for you to grab your eraser and make it disappear from your drawing.

Remember, the most important thing is to have fun and enjoy the process! Keep practicing and you'll be creating amazing drawings in no time!

Practice Drawing Lines

Before we start our art adventure, let's practice
drawing some awesome lines!

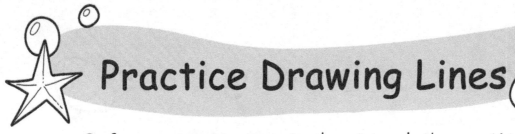

Practice Drawing Lines

Before we start our art adventure, let's practice
drawing some awesome lines!

Mermaids, Unicorns and More

Mermaid 1

Mermaid 2

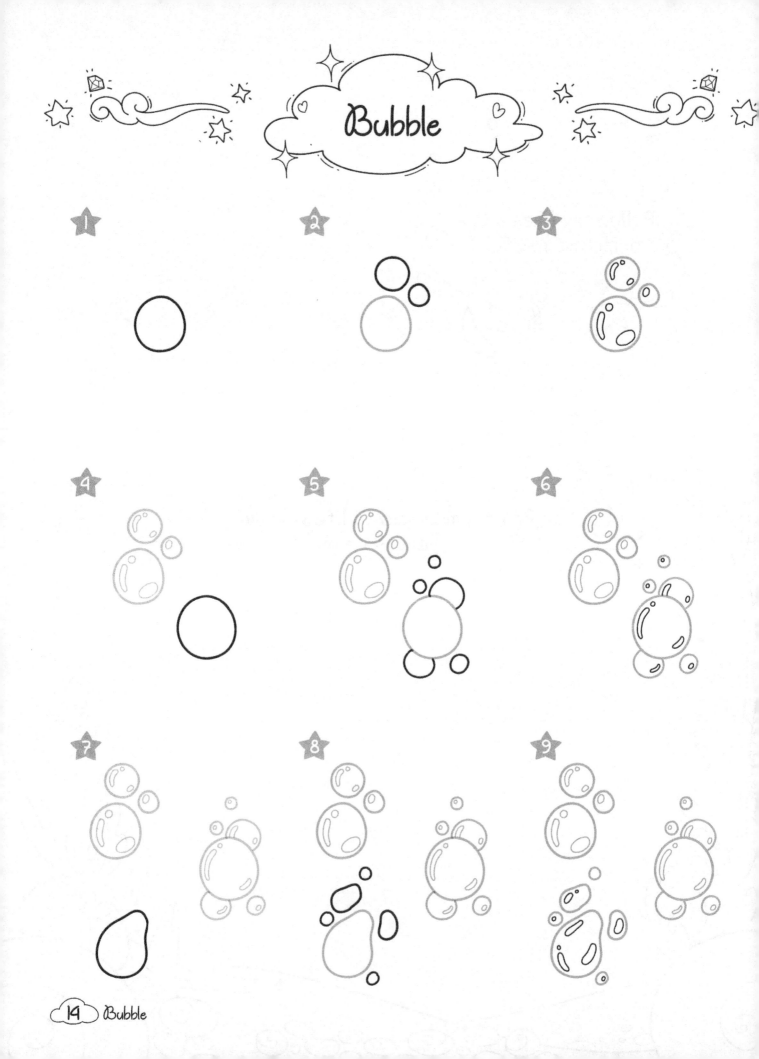

Bubble

Octopus

Follow my outline for a tracing challenge.

Let your imagination run wild as you create a mystical octopus

Jellyfish

Hone your skills with a trace of me.

Draw a mesmerizing jellyfish and explore the wonders of the ocean

Sea Turtle

Tang Fish

Narwhal

Trace my lines to sharpen your skills

Create a majestic narwhal and explore the wonders of the ocean

Sea Horse

Follow my outline for a tracing challenge.

Let your pencils take you on a journey to the mystical world of sea horses

Conch Shell

Hone your skills with a trace of me.

Capture the essence of the ocean by sketching a beautiful conch shell

Coral

Kraken

Follow my lines and bring me to life!

Unleash your creativity and create a mythical Kraken

Pearl

Trace my lines to sharpen your skills

Let's get creative and draw a beautiful pearl!

Dolphin

Follow my outline for a tracing challenge.

Let your imagination run wild as you draw an enchanting dolphin

Starfish

Hone your skills with a trace of me.

Embark on an underwater adventure and bring a starfish to life

Seaweed

Let me be your guide, trace and improve.

Experience the beauty of the ocean by sketching seaweed

Moon

Seagull

Whale

Follow my outline for a tracing challenge.

Let your artistic skills shine as you create a magnificent whale

Crab

Hone your skills with a trace of me.

Bring a cute crab to life and add some fun to your artwork

Kelp

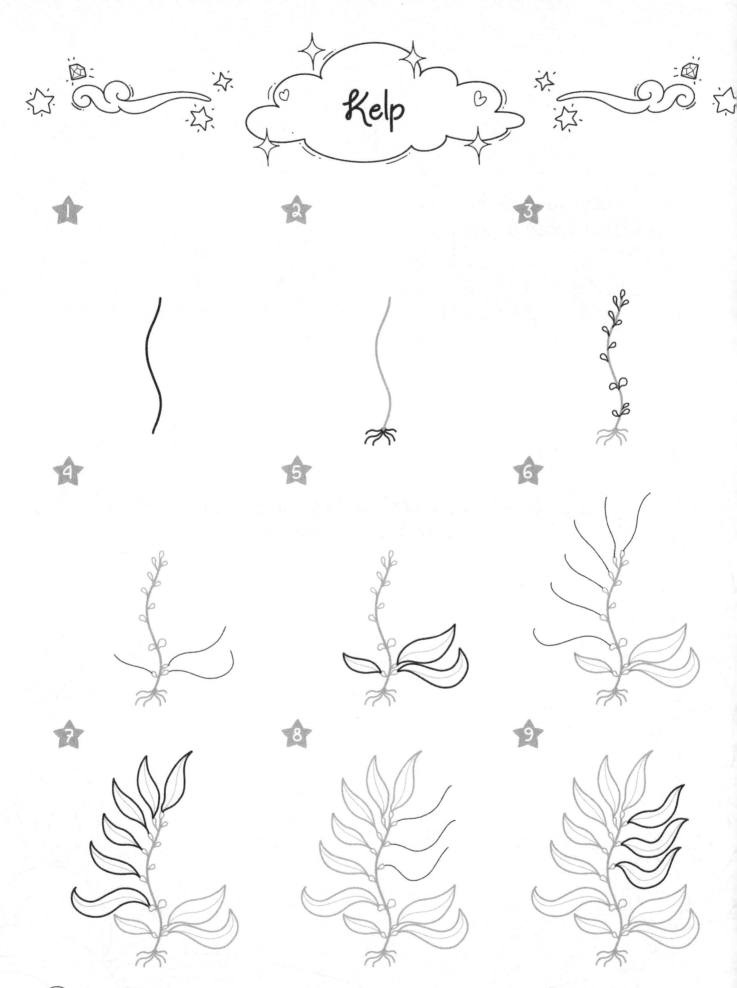

Let me be your guide, trace and improve.

Capture the essence of the ocean by sketching kelp

Mermaid 3

Trace my lines to sharpen your skills.

Let your creativity flow and sketch a mermaid

Mermaid 4

Follow my outline for a tracing challenge.

Unleash your creativity and bring a mermaid to life!

Merman

Hone your skills
with a trace of me.

Let your imagination soar as you create
a magical merman

Trident

Follow my lines and bring me to life!

Dive into the depths of creativity and craft a stunning trident

Triton
God of the Sea

1 2 3 4 5 6 7 8 9

Let me be your guide, trace and improve.

Summon the power of the sea as you bring Triton, the god of the sea, to li

Unicorn 1

Trace my lines to sharpen your skills.

Bring magic to life by creating a unicorn with your pencils

Unicorn 2

Follow my outline for a tracing challenge.

Create your own mystical creature with your pencils - a unicorn!

Unicorn 3

Hone your skills with a trace of me.

Let the magic begin as you create a magnificent unicorn

Baby Unicorn

Rainbow

Follow my lines and bring me to life!

Draw a stunning rainbow and bring some color to your artwork

Fairy

Trace my lines to sharpen your skills.

Let your imagination run wild as you create a charming fairy

Magical Dust

Follow my outline for a tracing challenge.

Create a magical dust around the wings of this charming fairy

Magic Wand

Hone your skills with a trace of me.

Craft a magic wand and make your artistic dreams come true

Mushroom House

Let me be your guide, trace and improve.

Build a whimsical mushroom house and explore the magic within

Peğasus

Follow my lines and bring me to life!

Create a magnificent Pegasus and soar into the world of fantasy

Golden Apple

Trace my lines to sharpen your skills.

Bring a golden apple to life and add some magic to your artwork

Alicorn

Follow my outline for a tracing challenge.

Unleash your creativity and create an enchanting Alicorn

Butterfly

Hone your skills with a trace of me.

Draw beautiful butterflies and add some elegance to your artwork

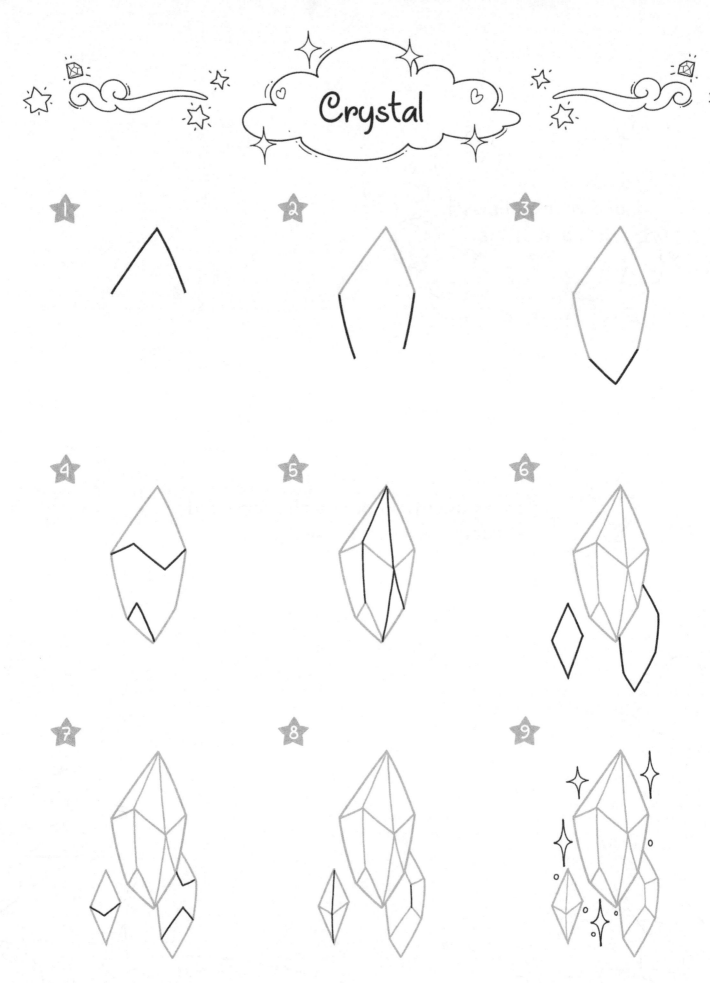

Crystal

Let me be your guide, trace and improve.

Create a stunning crystal and let it sparkle on the page

Lily

1 2 3
4 5 6
7 8 9

Follow my lines and bring me to life!

Draw delicate lilies and let their beauty inspire you

Sun

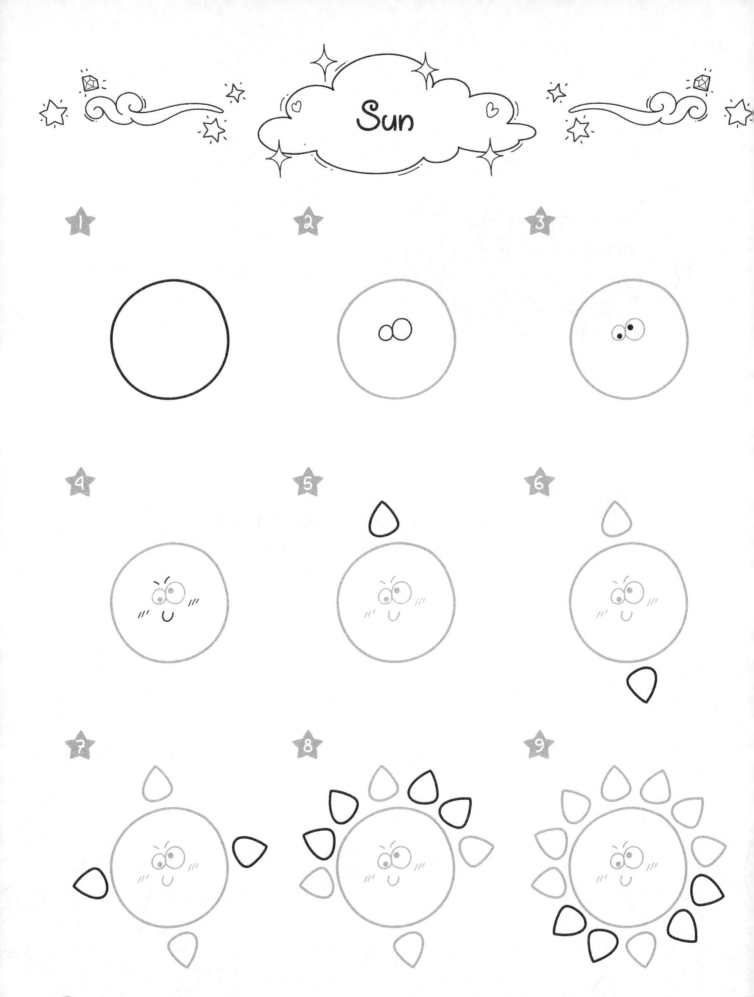

Trace my lines to sharpen your skills.

Let your imagination soar as you create a radiant sun

Shooting Star

Follow my outline for a tracing challenge.

Draw a mesmerizing shooting star and make a wish

Castle Tower

Hone your skills with a trace of me.

Build a castle tower and enter a world of royalty and magic

Princess

Let me be your guide, trace and improve.

Create a beautiful princess and let her story unfold

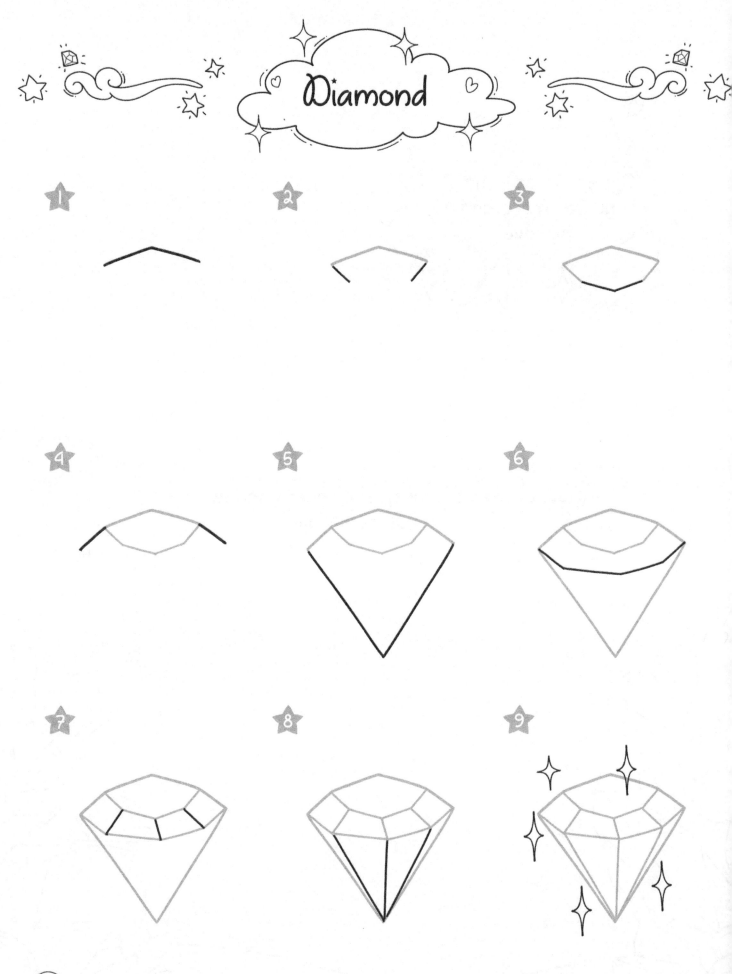

Follow my lines and bring me to life!

Bring a stunning diamond to life and let it shine on the page

Crown

Trace my lines to sharpen your skills.

Craft a royal crown and feel like a king or queen

Dragon

Follow my outline for a tracing challenge.

Unleash your creativity and create a fiery dragon

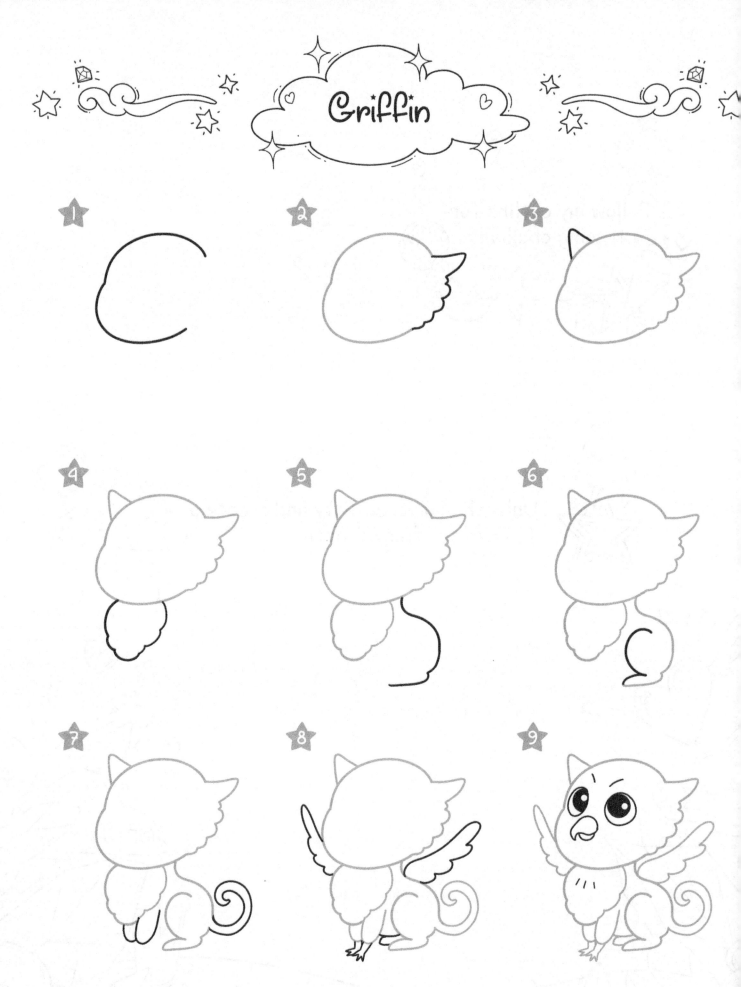

Griffin

Hone your skills with a trace of me.

Let your imagination run wild as you create a majestic griffin

Elf

Let me be your guide, trace and improve.

Draw a mystical elf and explore the wonders of fantasy

Pixie

1 2 3
4 5 6
7 8 9

110 Pixie

Follow my lines and bring me to life!

Create an enchanting pixie and let her magic inspire you

Phoenix

Trace my lines to sharpen your skills.

Bring a magnificent phoenix to life and let it soar on the page

Congratulations! You did it! You've completed the How to Draw Mermaids, Unicorns and More book! Your drawing skills have leveled up and we are so proud of you!

Drawing is such a fun and creative way to express yourself, and we hope this book has inspired you to keep practicing and improving your skills. Keep your pencils sharpened and your imagination flowing, because the world is full of magical creatures waiting to be drawn by you!

Remember, even the greatest artists started with a blank piece of paper and a pencil. It's all about taking the time to practice and experiment. Don't be afraid to try new things and let your creativity soar. We can't wait to see what amazing drawings you create next!

So, once again, congratulations on completing the How to Draw Mermaids, Unicorns and More book. You are now a certified drawing wizard! Keep on practicing and keep on creating!

Made in the USA
Monee, IL
28 November 2024

71520865R00063